Turtles

Melvin and Gilda Berger

SCHOLASTIC INC.

New York Toronto London Auckland Sydney
Mexico City New Delhi Hong Kong Buenos Aires

Photographs: Cover: S. Nielsen/Bruce Coleman Inc., New York; p. 1: S. Nielsen/Bruce Coleman Inc.; p. 3: Lynn M. Stone/Bruce Coleman Inc.; p. 4: Tom Brakefield/Bruce Coleman Inc.; p. 5: Charles V. Angelo/Photo Researchers, New York; p. 6: J. C. Carton/Bruce Coleman Inc.; p.7: Winland Rice/Bruce Coleman Inc.; p. 8: Gene Ahrens/Bruce Coleman Inc.; p. 9: C. W. Schwartz/Animals Animals, Chatham, NY; p. 10: Joe McDonald/Bruce Coleman Inc.; p. 11: Cosmos Blank/Photo Researchers; p. 12: E. R. Degginger/Photo Researchers; p. 13: Photo Researchers; p. 14: Tom & Pat Leeson/Photo Researchers; p. 15: Dale & Marian Zimmerman/Bruce Coleman Inc.; p. 16: Leonard Lee Rue III/Bruce Coleman Inc.

Book design by Annette Cyr

ISBN 0-439-44535-3

12   6 7/0

Printed in the U.S.A.
First printing, October 2002

It is fall.

Some turtles live on land.

Fun Fact
Turtles can live almost anywhere and eat many different foods.

Some turtles live in the sea.

Fun Fact

If in danger, most land turtles pull their heads and legs into their shells.

Land turtles have four legs.

Sea turtles have four flippers.

Fun Fact

Many land turtles sleep, or hibernate (HYE-bur-nate), in winter.

It is winter.

Most turtles sleep until spring.

It is spring.

Fun Fact

Both land and sea turtles make their nests on land. They lay from 1 to 200 eggs at a time.

All turtles lay their eggs on land.

The turtle eggs hatch.

Baby sea turtles run to the water.

It is summer.

Fun Fact

The turtles blend in with their surroundings.

Some turtles look like the ground.

Can you find the turtle?